I0821159

WHAT GOOD IS A DEAD TREE?

A Science Mystery

Doug Wechsler

Millbrook Press / Minneapolis

For Debbie with love.

Millbrook Press™
An imprint of Lerner Publishing Group, Inc.
241 First Avenue North
Minneapolis, MN 55401 USA

For reading levels and more information, look up this title at www.lernerbooks.com.

Diagram on page 31 by Laura K. Westlund.

Additional image credits: Vlad Antonov/Shutterstock, p. 2; xpixel/Shutterstock, pp. 3, 40; BSIP/UIG/Getty Images, p. 23 (right top); Zohaib Ur Rehman Afridi/Alamy, p. 23 (right middle); NNehring/Getty Images, p. 23 (right bottom); Wikimedia Commons PD, p. 25; Design elements: FrentaN/Shutterstock; cepera/Shutterstock.

Designed by Kimberly Morales.
Main body text set in Caecilia LT Std. Typeface provided by Adobe Systems.

Library of Congress Cataloging-in-Publication Data

Names: Wechsler, Doug author
Title: What good is a dead tree? : a science mystery / Doug Wechsler.
Description: Minneapolis, MN : Millbrook Press, [2026] | Includes bibliographical references and index. | Audience: Ages 9–14 | Audience: Grades 4–6 | Summary: "What happens to a tree after it falls in a forest? Dig into this biological mystery and explore how animals, insects, and fungi break down a fallen oak tree" —Provided by publisher.
Identifiers: LCCN 2025022315 (print) | LCCN 2025022316 (ebook) | ISBN 9798348010539 library binding | ISBN 9798348027865 epub
Subjects: LCSH: Forest ecology—Juvenile literature | Trees—Juvenile literature | Oak—Ecology—Juvenile literature
Classification: LCC QH541.5.F6 W397 2026 (print) | LCC QH541.5.F6 (ebook)

LC record available at https://lccn.loc.gov/2025022315
LC ebook record available at https://lccn.loc.gov/2025022316

Manufactured in the United States of America
1-1012840-57007-10/13/2025

CONTENTS

PROLOGUE

MYSTERIOUS DARK STRIPE

A tree has disappeared. You are a scientist. You must find out who made off with it and where it is now. To solve this mystery, you'll have to investigate beetles, flat bugs, and bizarre fungi.

Imagine that you're walking in the woods, and something catches your eye. A curious column of rotten wood the length of a telephone pole lies flush with the ground. Could that have been a tree? If so, where did it go? We will have to go back fifty years to when this tree was alive and work our way to the present to answer these questions. Along the way, we will meet springtails, farting termites, and an occasional snake and salamander. And we'll learn just how good a dead tree is. Together, we can solve the mystery of the disappearing tree.

These look like rotten wood chips.
Were they once a tree?

CHAPTER 1

UH-OH, BUTT ROT: FIFTY YEARS AGO

The big old oak is a busy place. Birds chirp among its branches, caterpillars chew on its leaves, and squirrels scurry up its trunk.

But this oak has a big problem—butt rot. A gross-looking mushroom is growing out of the base of the trunk. That means trouble inside the bottom of the tree. This mushroom is part of a fungus that is decaying wood within the tree. Inside the trunk, that fungus causes lots of rot as it breaks down cellulose and feeds on the wood. Cellulose is the main building block of wood that gives it its strength. By the time the mushroom appears, the tree may not have long to live.

How is this mushroom connected to the fungus that is killing the tree? It is part of the fungus. The fungus is made up of a network of tiny fibers. These connected fibers form a mycelium (my-SEE-lee-um). The mycelium is difficult to see inside a host tree. But if all the wood and bark disappeared, it would look like a huge net of tiny fibers.

The oak bracket fungus causes butt rot in trees that are otherwise healthy.

An eastern gray squirrel peers down from a mighty oak.

Buck moth caterpillars gather for safety on an oak leaf.

A Fungus Among Us

A fungus is a member of the kingdom of life that includes mushrooms, molds, and yeasts. You are probably familiar with the animal kingdom and plant kingdom. For a long time, scientists classified fungi as plants. But scientists were surprised when they studied the deoxyribonucleic acid (DNA) in fungi. DNA is a molecule that guides how each organism is made. Fungus DNA is more like an animal's DNA than a plant's. Think of it this way—a fungus is more closely related to humans than it is to a carrot! So, scientists created a new kingdom: Fungi.

Fungi live everywhere. We often don't pay attention to them unless they make our toes itch (athlete's foot), turn our bread green (bread mold), or top our pizza (mushrooms). Fungi in logs break down the wood and feed many of the animals that live in a log. Organisms that break down and recycle dead plants and animals and other organic matter are called decomposers. They play a huge role in logs, as well as everywhere else on our planet.

Green spores grow from bread mold.

This mycelium, the body of a fungus, grows inside a rotten log.

Mushrooms add extra flavor to pizza.

The mycelium is the body of the fungus. It can live for years inside a tree. Mushrooms are short-lived fruiting bodies that grow out of the hidden mycelium. A mycelium is sort of like an apple tree, and the mushroom is like the apple. To produce this large mushroom, the mycelium used the nutrients it gained from breaking down the tree's cellulose, thus weakening the tree.

One day, a summer storm roars through the forest, causing even sturdy trees to sway. A blast of wind bashes the butt-rotted oak and fractures the base of its trunk. With a loud series of sputtering cracks, gravity brings the windblown tree crashing to the ground. *BOOM!* The impact crushes many branches.

Rest in peace, old oak tree. Birds have flown, squirrels have fled, and caterpillars were catapulted from their leaves. Now a new cast of characters will take over.

The life of the tree is ending, but the fallen tree will be teeming with life again. Soon a new group of animals will call this new log home and help it to disappear over the next few decades. It's your job to investigate where the tree goes.

This dead oak tree will soon be full of life.

CHAPTER 2

PIONEERS OF DECAY: FORTY-NINE YEARS AGO

A year has passed. The fallen tree has died, and it is now officially a log. The log is still sprawled out on the forest floor. It doesn't look as if it's gone anywhere. But take a closer look. Your first clue is a tiny plug of sawdust spilling out of the fallen trunk. Where did it come from? Bark beetles.

Why did the bark beetles suddenly show up? They sensed alcohol in the air. The impact of the falling tree cracked the bark. Microscopic bacteria floating in the air landed on the bark.

Rain washed them into the cracks. Beneath the bark of the damaged tree, bacteria converted sugars in the tree's sap into alcohol. The alcohol wafts into the air. Tiny bark beetles sense the alcohol with their antennae and fly toward it. Why? The alcohol signals to beetles that a tree is dying. And a dying tree provides the food for bark beetle larvae.

A female bark beetle's first task is to bore a hole through the bark and into the wood. From the outside, all you see is a plug of sawdust. Inside the hole, she lays eggs. When the eggs hatch, the larvae feed beneath the bark. What do the larvae chow down on? The cambium—the thin, nutritious layer between the bark and the wood where the growth of the trunk took place.

The hole that the bark beetle chewed into the cambium is also a portal for fungi. How does this happen? Microscopic spores of fungi float in the air.

A tiny bark beetle tunnels into the fallen oak to start a new generation.

As bark beetles chew tunnels into the recently fallen tree, sawdust piles up at the tunnel entrances.

Layers of a Tree Trunk

As a tree grows, the trunk becomes wider with each new layer of bark. Take a look at the different layers of a tree trunk.

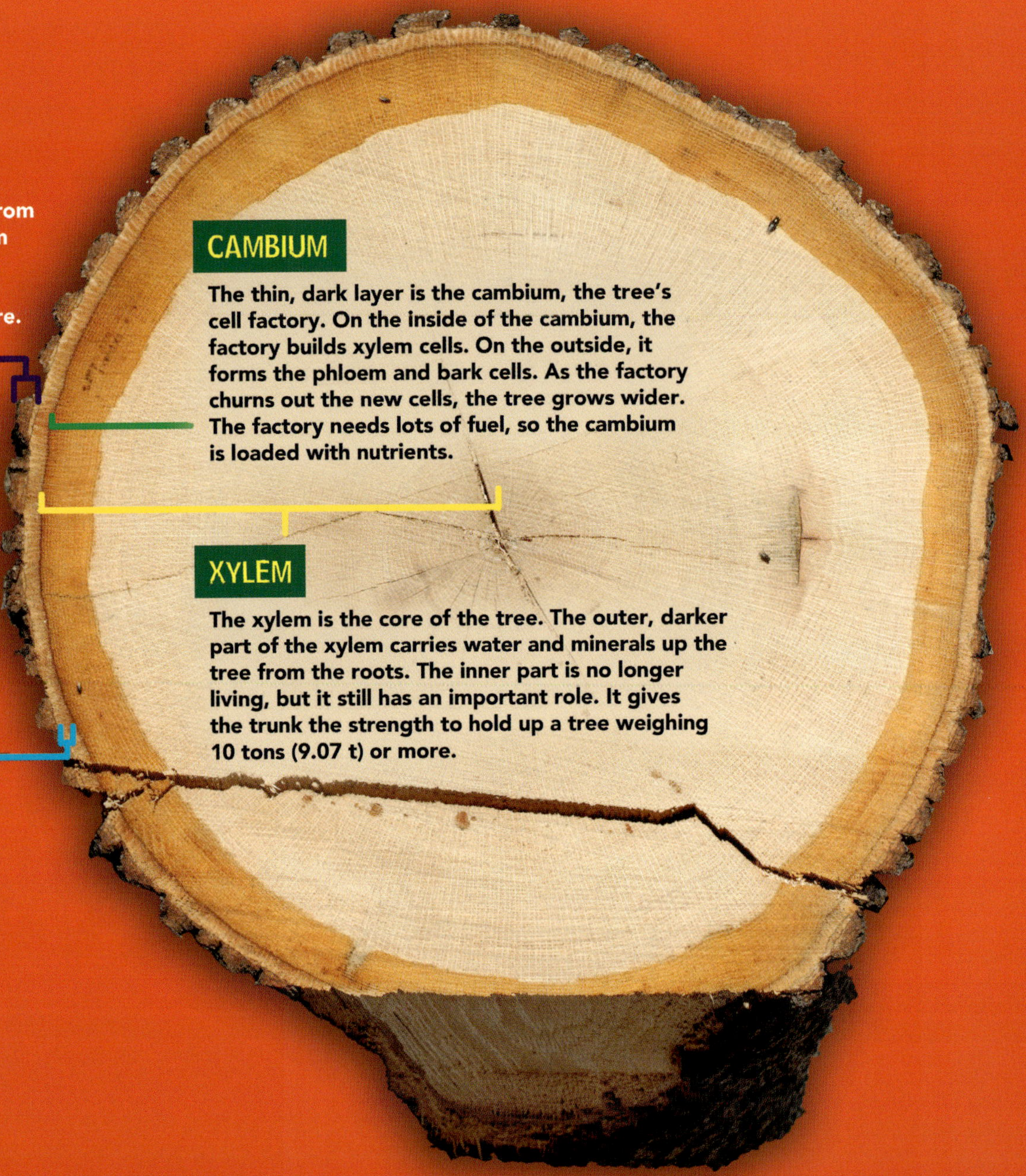

OUTER BARK

The tough outer bark is made from dead phloem, which comes from the layer just beneath the bark. Bark shields the tree against fungus, insects, drought, and fire.

CAMBIUM

The thin, dark layer is the cambium, the tree's cell factory. On the inside of the cambium, the factory builds xylem cells. On the outside, it forms the phloem and bark cells. As the factory churns out the new cells, the tree grows wider. The factory needs lots of fuel, so the cambium is loaded with nutrients.

PHLOEM

Phloem in the trunk acts like a bundle of tiny pipes in which sap flows to the roots. The sap contains sugar and nutrients made in the leaves using the energy of the sun.

XYLEM

The xylem is the core of the tree. The outer, darker part of the xylem carries water and minerals up the tree from the roots. The inner part is no longer living, but it still has an important role. It gives the trunk the strength to hold up a tree weighing 10 tons (9.07 t) or more.

One spore drifts into the tunnel that the bark beetle bored into the cambium. A few days later, a new fungus sprouts from the spore. It starts as a slender strand almost too skinny to see. As it grows, the fungus feeds on the cambium. But unlike an animal, it digests its food outside its "body." It oozes out chemicals called enzymes to break down the cambium and then soaks up the nutrients. As the fungus eats away at the cambium, a space opens beneath the bark. Cracks in the bark create a gateway for more animals and fungi to enter the rotting cambium.

Bark beetles and fungi aren't the only organisms chowing down in the cambium. One common critter of the cambium is the fire-colored beetle. It lays its eggs beneath a loose piece of bark. When the larva hatches, it's like a flattened mealworm. Its shape fits nicely in the narrow space beneath the bark. Scientists are divided about whether the larva eats rotten wood and fungi in the cambium or preys on other insects that eat the cambium. In either case, it gets its nutrients indirectly from the cambium. It can take anywhere from a few weeks to several months for the larva to grow to be almost 1 inch (2.5 cm) long.

Fungus Spores

Fungi reproduce by making spores for the same reason plants make seeds. A whole new fungus grows from a single spore. Spores can be made of one or a few cells. They are tiny—a huge spore would be the width of a human hair. Spores may travel on the wind or stick to the body of an animal. This helps spread the fungus to new locations.

Do you want to see these spores yourself? Place the cap of a wild mushroom, without the stalk, on a piece of white paper and leave it for a day. Spores falling out of the mushroom will form a pattern that resembles the underside of the mushroom. This is called a spore print.

The soft-bodied fire-colored beetle larva is easy prey for centipedes that have a similar flattened form.

Then it molts and becomes a pupa, a stage of metamorphosis in which the animal looks a little like a pale, alien insect. After emerging from the pupa, the adult beetle has wings and it flies off to feed on nectar and pollen from flowers. Did a part of the tree fly off with the beetle?

The beetle will go on to find a mate, and the female will lay her eggs in another dead tree, starting the cycle all over again.

In the space beneath the bark, other flat creatures creep along, foraging for food. Centipedes hunt for larvae. Flat bugs feast on fungi. Red flat bark beetles prey on the larvae of other beetles. Slender millipedes munch rotting bits of the cambium, decomposing insects, and fungus.

Tiny white flecks that look like dandruff also move in the dark beneath the bark. Through a magnifying glass, you can see that they are springtails—tiny, six-legged animals that are abundant in moist, dark places. Many springtails don't even grow to 0.04 inches (1 mm) long. Springtails come in many colors and shapes. They feed on fungus that

The eyes and antennae form as the fire-colored beetle larva pupates.

The adult fire-colored beetle spends little time in the log before flying off.

Tiny springtails are among the most abundant animals beneath the bark.

is consuming the log and detritus, decaying bits of plants and animals.

Wood is tough stuff, but fungi, beetles, and springtails slowly break it down. After a year on the ground, the fallen tree looks like it is still all there, but a tiny part has already disappeared. Sugars in the cambium were converted into alcohol and drifted into the air. Sawdust from bark fell to the ground as bark beetles tunneled. Fungi consumed parts of the log. And springtails and beetle larvae fed on those fungi.

A springtail crawls through fungus, its main food source.

CHAPTER 3

BUSY, BUSY LOG: FORTY-SEVEN YEARS AGO

Three years after the tree toppled, all but the biggest branches have been weakened by the many decomposers and have broken off. The bark is loose. Fungi have begun growing in the xylem, rotting the wood. The soft wood allows other organisms to move deeper into the log as well. The log is like a bustling apartment building with different occupants on each level.

In the fall, a number of mycelia growing inside the log are ready to grow mushrooms—their fruiting bodies. One particularly beautiful mushroom is called yellow fairy cups.

Like many other mushrooms, it lasts only a few days. It creates spores and decomposes, but the mycelium lives on, unseen inside the log. Many mycelia form mushrooms once a year.

Fungi put the *rot* in rotten wood. More and more fungi invade the log lying on the forest floor. The fungi spread almost invisibly through the log. Fungi provide food for insects and other invertebrates invading the rotting log. As fungi decay the wood, more animals can tunnel through it.

One of these insects is a young queen carpenter ant. The ant flies until it finds a suitable place to nest—such as this fallen tree. Shedding her wings, the large black ant shimmies through a crack in the bark and hollows out a chamber in the soft wood. This queen will spend the rest of her life in the log.

The queen lays two dozen eggs and cares for the larvae after they hatch. Her fat and muscles break down to provide nutrients for her and her offspring. The pudgy white larvae feed on secretions from inside the queen's mouth. Even while the larvae spin cocoons and pupate, she stays in the chamber guarding them, still without a bite to eat. When the pupae develop into adult ants, the queen helps them break free of their cocoons.

Purple jellydisc (*left*) and yellow fairy cups (*right*) grow from their mycelia in the oak log.

Life Stages of Insects

Insects have two different ways of growing up. Some go through three life stages, and some go through four. The change from one life stage to another is called metamorphosis.

Insects with three life stages start out as an egg, hatch into a nymph, and then become an adult. The nymph often looks much like the adult but without wings. Cockroaches, stink bugs, and crickets have three life stages.

Insects with four life stages go from egg to larva to pupa to adult. Insects reach their full size during the larval stage. Beyond that, they change shape but don't grow larger. Caterpillars and beetle grubs are larvae. The pupa is the resting stage. Inside the pupa, the body rearranges into what will become the adult stage. When the insect crawls out of the pupal skin, it becomes an adult that looks nothing like the larva. Ants, bees, beetles, flies, and moths belong to this group.

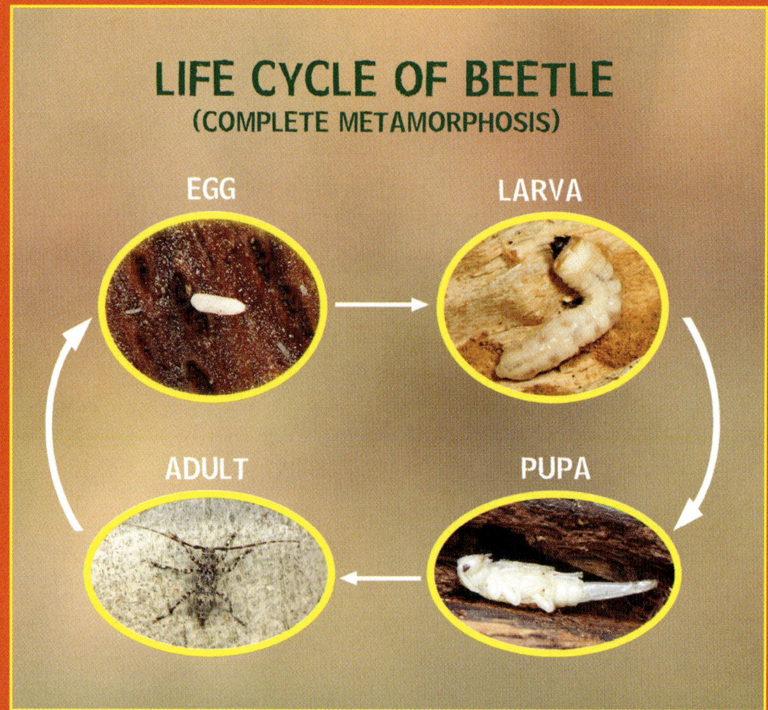

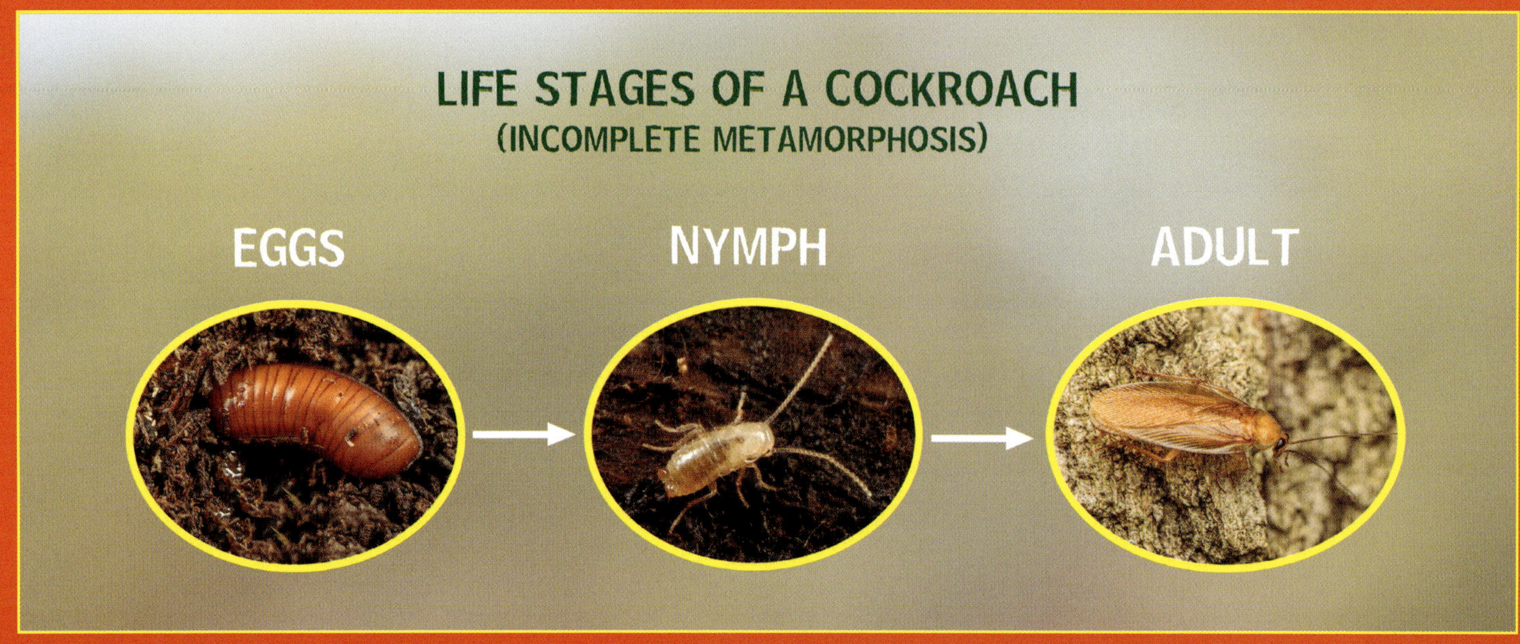

A new carpenter ant queen cares for her eggs, larvae, and pupae.

Tunneling carpenter ants speed up the decomposition of the log.

Soon the ants foray from the chamber to forage for living and dead insects and honeydew—the sweet poop of aphids. They return, bringing their devoted queen her first meal in ten weeks. From here on, the queen's only duty will be to lay eggs. Her offspring will do all the rest of the work.

Carpenter ants carve tunnels through the middle of the log with their powerful jaws. The ants don't eat the wood. Instead, they create spaces to raise the young and passageways for safe travel. Many other creatures will take advantage of these dark highways. The chewed-up bits of the tree become sawdust that, with the help of other creatures, will turn into soil.

At the other end of the log, a horned passalus beetle family tunnels through the rotten wood. The parents and older offspring take care of the young grubs. This sort of family life is rare among insects. If other passalus beetles intrude on their rotten log, these beetles will defend their territory.

Beetles and other tunnel builders do a great service for the log ecosystem. The half-inch-wide (1.3 cm) tunnel of the passalus becomes a freeway for bees, wasps, spiders, salamanders, millipedes, centipedes, and other creatures that cannot build their own tunnels. In addition, fungal spores often stick to the animals. The spores get a free ride deeper into the log to grow new mycelia and soften more wood.

Unlike most beetles, horned passalus beetles make sounds to communicate with family members.

The only hornets to survive the winter are young queens, which often shelter in rotten wood.

Beetles make up the most diverse group of insects in logs. In one North Carolina study, scientists found more than fifty species of beetles in oak logs. They uncovered as many types of beetles in the logs as all other kinds of insects combined.

Tunnels and soft wood aid animals seeking shelter for the winter. Before frost sets in, a queen hornet homes in on the oak log. She enters through an old beetle burrow. Then she creeps into the log and creates a cozy chamber. Dangling by her feet, she enters a deep sleep. She doesn't move all winter. Hanging in her hollow, her body touches nothing but air. This is important because just touching ice that forms inside the log could spread ice crystals into the hornet's body. Ice crystals can be deadly because water expands when it freezes, which would burst the cells that make up the hornet's body.

A fire-colored beetle larva also prepares for winter. Ice crystals can form around bacteria, so it empties its gut to get rid of them. The larva also produces a protein that acts as antifreeze. The protein flows with fluids through the larva's body. Then the insect can withstand temperatures down to –4°F (–20°C) without becoming a bugsicle.

A fallen log cools more slowly than the surrounding ground in winter and stays cooler in summer. Many small animals hide inside logs in winter where wood prevents sudden freezing.

After winter passes and spring returns, a fungus gnat lays eggs in the rotten log. A couple of weeks later, a soft spot in the log seethes with fungus gnat larvae. These maggots munch detritus, fungus, and frass (chewed wood and insect droppings). The maggots are transparent, so you can see the food in their guts. When that comes out the other end, it will feed fungi and bacteria. Then other animals will eat the poop along with the fungi and bacteria. Every journey through a creature's gut is another step toward creating soil from wood.

While fungus gnat larvae gnaw on mycelia, mushrooms from those fungi grow out of the log. Some are quite tasty. Deer, squirrels, and chipmunks dine on the mushrooms. As these animals continue to wander around the forest, they scatter spore-filled scat (droppings). If that scat splats onto another log, those spores may grow into fungi and thrive there as well. Spores also stick to the bodies of beetles, flies, and slugs that munch on mushrooms. These spores may hitch a ride to another nearby log as well.

Meanwhile, a pileated woodpecker hammers away at the rotting log looking for a meal. Wood chips fly with each blow. The bird eats the fat larvae of horned passalus beetles, longhorn beetles, and other insects.

The trunk of the fallen tree looks as large as ever, but the tree is decomposing. What is missing after the first few years, and where has it gone? Tunneling carpenter ants and horned passalus beetles have turned parts of the log into sawdust and frass. Fungus gnats helped make soil from bits of the log, and woodpeckers chipped away, scattering shards of wood.

No bird does more than the pileated woodpecker to break down logs. It leaves behind large holes in dead tree trunks.

Fungus gnat larvae feed for a week or two before pupating.

CHAPTER 4

SOGGY LOG: FORTY YEARS AGO

After a decade, decomposers have decayed the oak into a mushy brown log riddled with holes. The spongy wood soaks up water. Carpenter ants are gone, but their tunnels have left part of the log hollow.

After a heavy rain, what seems like smoke streams out of a nearby rotting tree stump. It's actually a swarm of flying termites, each with two pairs of wings twice the length of its body. A male and female termite land on the oak log. They scurry to the ground, scrape off their wings, and scramble into the soil next to the log. The pair mates, and the female lays eggs. They are now king and queen termites. Both members of the royal couple care for their brood until their offspring are old enough to care for them. From then on, the queen's only work will be to lay eggs. The male's only job will be to mate with the queen. They may live for more than a decade.

As the queen and king continue producing new generations, their offspring tunnel into the log and chow down on it. They can't digest their woody diet on their own. That's because wood is mostly made of tough cellulose. The termites get help from a busy community of microbes—single-celled organisms—in their guts. These helpers break down cellulose in chewed-up wood into smaller chemicals that termites can digest.

Winged termite adults will soon fly off to seek mates.

The Smallest Decomposers

In addition to the kingdoms of plants, animals, and fungi, three other major divisions of life dwell inside logs: bacteria, archaea, and protists. The creatures in these groups are all single-celled organisms, and they're the most abundant life-forms on Earth. Members of these groups help to break down the log into food other organisms can use. (And some of them also live in termite guts!) Because they are microscopic, these organisms are also known as microbes. These tiny organisms play a huge role in decomposition.

- Bacteria come in many different shapes and sizes. If you lined them up end to end, between one hundred and one thousand could fit single file across the width of the period at the end of this sentence. Bacteria are found just about everywhere. In logs they especially thrive in frass, dead animals, and newly formed soil inside logs.

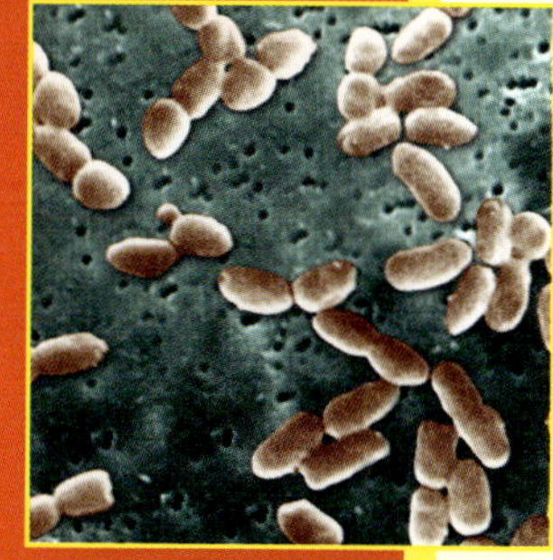

- Archaea (ar-KEY-uh) are similar in size to bacteria. Most look like bacteria as well. But they differ from bacteria in the makeup of their cell wall and the way they make protein. Many archaea live in extreme environments such as hot springs, oil wells, or the guts of termites.

- Protists are generally much larger than bacteria and archaea. They also differ in having a nucleus, a part that controls many of the functions inside the cell. In logs, protists live in animals' guts, in wet wood, and inside lichens (plantlike organisms) on the bark.

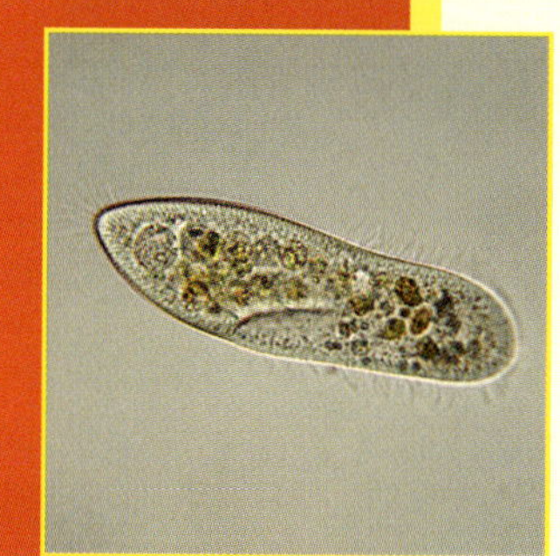

A colony of eastern subterranean termites may include up to a million workers.

Carolina mantleslugs slide through passageways beneath the bark.

Most waste that is not digested exits the termites as poop. But the bacteria also produce methane gas, which termites fart out, sending what was once part of the tree into the air.

Termites must molt their exoskeletons (tough skinlike coverings) as they grow. When a termite molts, it also sheds the lining of its gut. Out go its microbial partners! The termite regrows its gut lining, but how does it get its cellulose-eating partners back? It eats microbe-rich poop straight from the behinds of other termites!

Soggy logs are an important habitat for animals that need moisture—or a place to hide. Sliding along its slime trail, a Carolina mantleslug slips through hollows in the log. Land snails and slugs are terrestrial (land-dwelling) mollusks that breathe through gills. Moisture is vital for mollusks. Their gills must stay wet for mollusks to breathe. Snails keep moist by sealing themselves inside their shells during dry weather. Slugs, snail relatives without shells to hide in, take shelter in damp places. Carolina mantleslugs spend most of their time inside rotten logs but may come out on rainy nights. They feed mainly on fungi, and they also slurp slime molds.

The Weird and Wonderful Life Cycle of a Slime Mold

What is slime mold? It looks like a fungus but isn't one. It creeps through the log, but it's not an animal. It creates fruiting bodies but isn't a plant. Instead, scientists classify slime mold as a protist. It leads a strange life.

Slime mold starts life emerging from a spore as a microscopic amoeba or as a flagellate. The amoeba will grow and divide into two amoebae. They continue to divide until two or more amoebae find each other. Then they combine to form a plasmodium. A flagellate also fuses with another flagellate to become a plasmodium. The plasmodium is a shape-shifting blob that grows and moves. It can creep at about 0.04 inches (1 mm) per second. That's just fast enough to detect with your eyes.

When food runs out, the blob flows to the outside of the log. There it separates into fruiting bodies. Depending on the species, these may look like brown bananas on black stalks, red lollipops, or yellow dog vomit. Spores form inside the fruiting body called the sporangium. Eventually, the sporangium dies and dries up and the spores blow in the wind or stick to animals. If they end up in a moist place, amoebas or flagellates will emerge from the spores and the cycle will begin again.

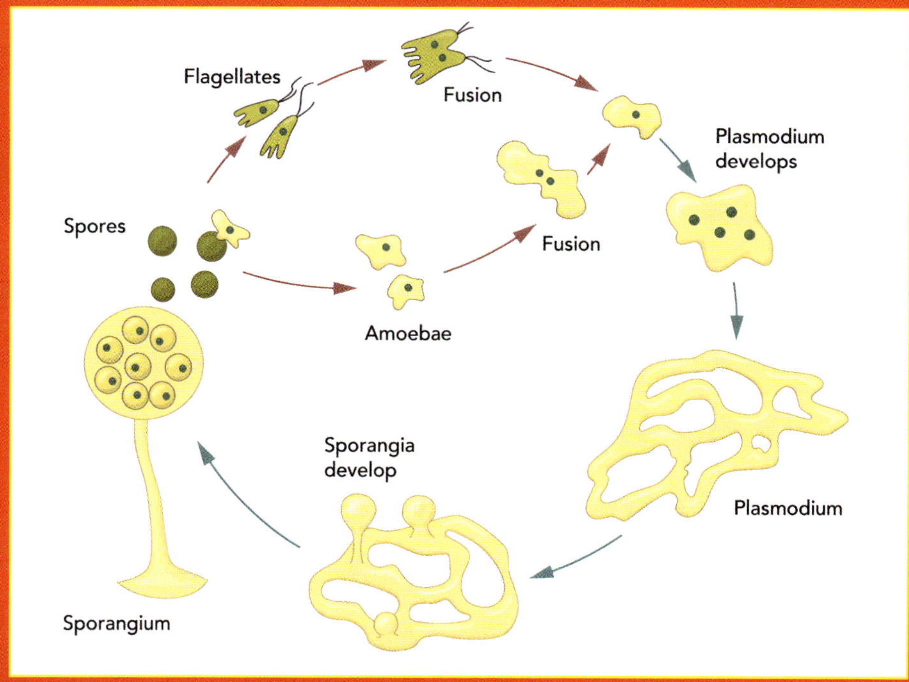

Chocolate tube slime mold

Hemitrichia

Dog vomit slime mold

A slime mold plasmodium creeps through a log, feeding as it goes.

Eastern red-backed salamanders prey on springtails, beetle larvae, and other tiny log dwellers.

A yellow slime mold slithers slowly through the rotten log. It looks like lemon-colored snot. As it moves, it devours detritus, fungus, and bacteria. In turn, it may be consumed by beetles, flies, and fungi.

Inside the soggy log, a red-backed salamander waits out the day. It needs to stay in moist places because it breathes through its skin and mouth lining. It has no lungs. Oxygen can only pass through the skin if it is damp. On a rainy night, it will step out for a bite of springtail, beetle, or mite.

Nearby, its mortal enemy, a ring-necked snake, also rests inside the log. In addition to swallowing salamanders, this snake scarfs down slugs and earthworms in the moist log. Although snakes and salamanders don't do much to decompose a log, the nutrients in their food originated in the log.

Speaking of moisture, what role does rain play in the disappearing log? What happens when a rainstorm pounds down on a log that has lost its bark and has lots of chewed-up bits lying on the surface? These bits are washed down into the soil and help to shrink the log.

After the first decade of decay, decomposition slows down. Decomposers have eaten the most nutritious parts of the log. For the next forty years, fungi continue to eat away at the log, though at a slower pace. Termites eat and tunnel through it. The shrinking log continues to provide shelter for salamanders, spiders, beetles, hibernating wasp queens, and other small creatures.

The secretive ring-necked snake often hides in logs.

CHAPTER 5

THE DISAPPEARING ACT: BACK TO THE PRESENT

After the first decade, the log decomposes very slowly. Decomposers have eaten all the best parts. Now, fifty years after the tree fell, you find that almost nothing is left of the huge oak. A brown stripe of soft, crumbling wood stretches across the forest floor where the tree fell. The average lifespan (or should we say death span) of a fallen oak log is shorter than the average lifespan of a person.

So how did the fallen tree disappear? Who are the culprits? Give it some thought before you read on!

The first thing to notice is that when the tree crashed to the ground, many branches were crushed and broke off the tree. Gravity was the culprit here.

The next piece of evidence was the sawdust coming out of the bark beetle tunnels. As the sawdust fell to the ground, a tiny bit of the log entered the soil. The tunneling activity of carpenter ants, beetles, and termites broke down the wood some more. As the woodpecker chipped away, pieces of log flew to the ground.

Bits of log also have moved through the food web. Fungi broke down cellulose and consumed it. The fungus-infested wood fed fungus gnat larvae. The gnats grew up and flew off, carrying molecules originally from the log. Deer ate mushrooms that grew from mycelia in the decomposing log. The deer wandered to another part of the forest. There they pooped out undigested parts of those mushrooms. A ring-necked snake swallowed a red-backed salamander that had eaten a springtail that had munched some slime mold that had once fed on fungus that grew in the log. Swarms of termites that grew up eating the log flew off to mate.

Molecules Matter

All substances are made of molecules. Some examples of molecules include water, carbon dioxide, and sugar. All molecules are made of atoms. For example, water (H_2O) has two atoms of hydrogen and one atom of oxygen. Chemical changes, such as digestion, rearrange the atoms to form new molecules with different properties. For instance, when a sugar molecule is digested, the sugar molecule is broken apart. After a series of chemical reactions, atoms from the sugar end up in molecules of water and carbon dioxide.

A vivid metallic ground beetle hunts in the last remains of the log.

Their bodies were built using wood that was once part of the log, so as they leave, they take part of the log with them.

Believe it or not, a lot of the log has also disappeared into the air. Wood is made mostly of carbon, hydrogen, and oxygen atoms. Atoms are the building blocks of molecules. As fungi, bacteria, and other decomposers consume wood, frass, and dead insects, they give off carbon dioxide (CO_2). CO_2 is a gas made of carbon from the log and oxygen from the air. So, as wood decomposes, carbon from the log floats into the air as CO_2.

Hydrogen from the wood combines with oxygen inside the bodies of decomposers as they digest their food. This forms water (H_2O). That water exits their bodies when they breathe, pee, and poop, or when they are eaten by a predator. Then, the hydrogen atoms in the water are no longer part of the log.

Much of the log has been turned into humus—the dark, nutrient-rich part of soil made from dead organisms and living microbes. Bacteria and fungi cause the wood to rot, which allows many small animals to eat it. Termites, worms, beetle larvae, and many other organisms eat rotting wood, and their poop becomes part of the humus. Worms eat humus in the rotting log, carry it belowground, and poop it out, making the soil richer. Humus improves the soil so that plants can grow better.

Your investigation is complete. It was the decomposers that have broken down the log. They were the driving force making the log disappear. Without decomposers, the world might be covered with dead wood. They return nutrients to the soil and create space for new life to grow. Decomposers keep our ecosystems healthy by recycling nutrients from the dead organisms to feed living ones. The tree has disappeared, but along the way the rotten wood became a really good home for so much life.

It's always a surprise to see earthworms beneath the bark of a log several feet above the ground.

The Carbon Cycle

Carbon is one of the key elements of life. Carbon moves around the environment in different forms. Scientists call this the carbon cycle. Carbon is one of the main building blocks of wood. When logs rot or trees grow, carbon changes form. Here are key parts of the carbon cycle.

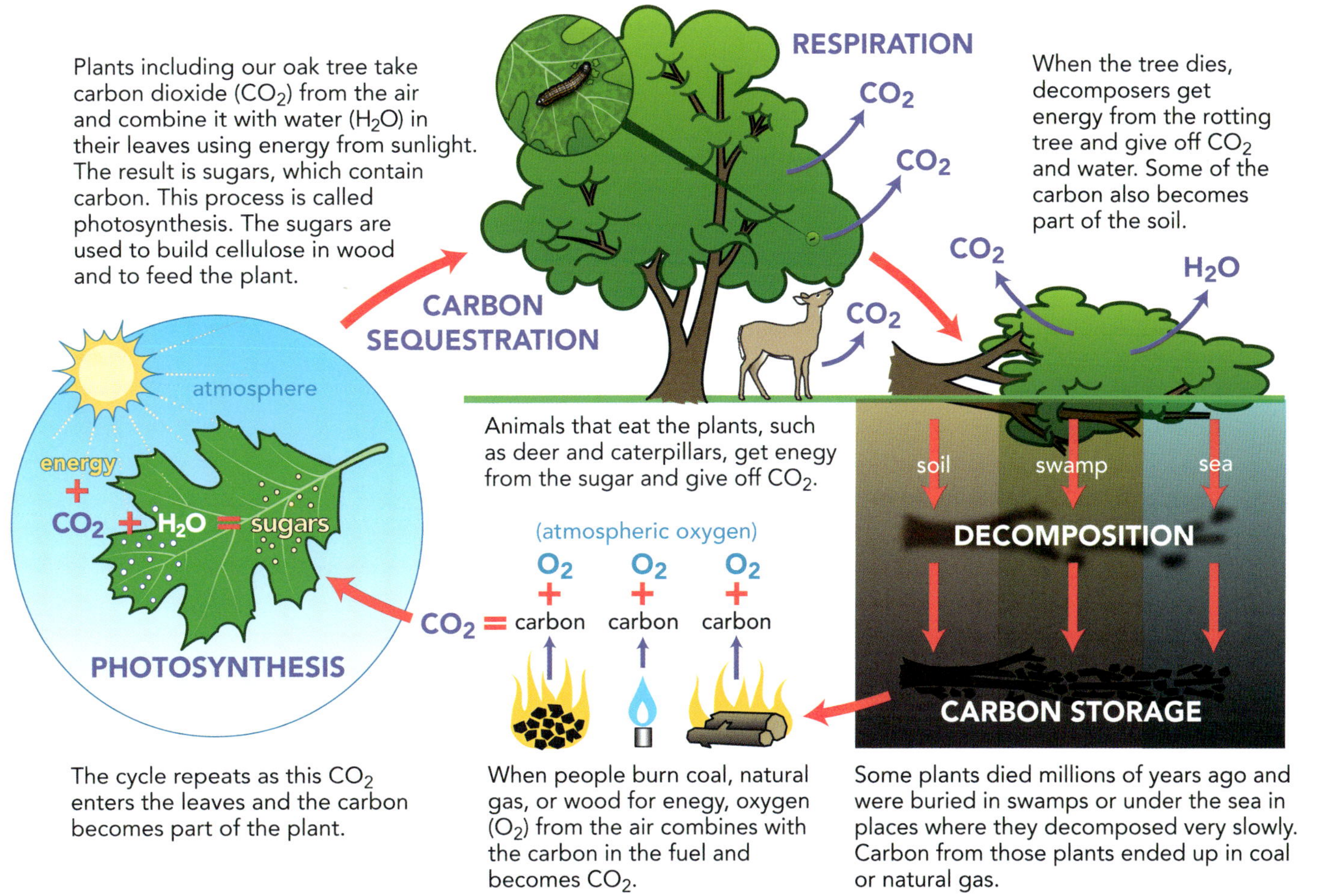

REBIRTH

A chipmunk stuffs an acorn into its cheek pouch. It buries the seed in its burrow beside the last bits of the rotten log. The acorn sprouts. Thanks to decomposers, nutrients in the soil that came from the oak log feed the oak seedling. The seedling grows bigger and bigger and bigger. After many years, a mighty oak stands where another fell. The cycle of life continues.

A chipmunk can stuff up to four acorns into its cheek pouches.

An oak seedling sprouts beside a rotten log.

A SUMMARY OF WHERE THE TREE WENT

YEAR 1 TO 3

- The impact of the fall knocks off some branches.
- Without food, the leaves die and fall to the ground.
- Bacteria turn sugars from the log into alcohol, and it evaporates into the air.
- Bark beetles bore into the tree, pushing out plugs of sawdust, which fall to the ground.
- Fungi consume much of the nutritious cambium. Beetle larvae eat fungus, then after pupating, turn into adults and fly off. Since they ate the fungus that consumed the cambium, they take molecules that made up the cambium with them.

YEAR 4 TO 9

- Fungi go deep into the log, penetrating the xylem. Mushrooms, the fruiting bodies of the fungi, pop out of the tree. When deer, squirrels, and slugs eat them, the animals carry the nutrients from xylem elsewhere.
- Carpenter ants chew tunnels through the log creating sawdust, which falls out or is carried out of the log and ends up in the soil.
- A pileated woodpecker hammers away at loose wood to get at beetle grubs. Pieces of rotten wood and bark fly to the ground.
- With the cambium gone, the bark is now loose. Bacteria and fungi get in the cracks and decay the weakest parts of the bark. Pieces of the bark start to fall off the log.

YEAR 10 TO 50

- Without the bark to protect it, rain washes bits of sawdust and frass from the log into the soil.
- Termites eat rotten wood in the log. Bacteria in their guts digest the wood and turn some of it into methane that the termite farts out. Poof! Now part of the tree is in the air. Termite poop ends up in the soil.

- Bacteria in the log also turn rotting wood into methane, carbon dioxide, and water.
- Worms consume rotting wood with fungi and poop it out. Sooner or later, that ends up in the soil.

LOGS IN THE GARDEN

In addition to the many decomposers you read about earlier, other animals also use logs for shelter. If you have a large garden or schoolyard, you can add logs to provide habitat for many types of creatures. Bumblebees nest inside logs with small hollows and can then pollinate your vegetables. Rat snakes find shelter inside the hollows and eat mice. Woodpeckers may visit to peck out beetle grubs. You will have your own laboratory to learn about ecology, the science of how plants and animals relate to one another and their environment.

Just don't put the logs close to your house or other structures! Termites, which are so valuable to the forest, may move in and nibble on your home.

INVESTIGATING ROTTEN LOGS

Studying life in logs can be fun, but you must be careful not to disturb the habitat too much. A good way to see many interesting log creatures is to look beneath logs by rolling them over. Do this with an adult who is aware of any hazards in the area. Also, check for yellowjackets, which sometimes nest in a rotten log, before turning it over. Be sure to roll the log back as soon as you are done. If you want to see what lives beneath the bark or deep inside a log, find someone who has a woodpile with logs that will be burned anyway. Replace any bark you peel away, so that the animals beneath it can survive.

A good magnifying lens will help you to see some of the smaller inhabitants of the log such as springtails. Some of these are so small that you may need a microscope to get a good view.

Bring along a small notebook and writing utensil, and you can keep a list of life-forms you find in the log.

A honeycomb coral slime mold fruiting body forms on the outside of the log.

Newborn sow bug hunters surround the mother spider.

As a larva, this fungus gnat grew up eating fungus decomposing a log.

GLOSSARY

amoeba (uh-MEE-bah): a single-celled organism that moves about shifting its shape

archaea (ar-KEE-uh): a group of simple, single-celled organisms, similar in size to bacteria but differing in the makeup of the cell wall and other characteristics

bacterium (back-TEER-ee-uhm): a simple, single-celled life-form without a nucleus; plural, bacteria

cambium (KAM-bee-um): the narrow layer between the xylem and the phloem where the growth of the trunk takes place

cell (SELL): the building block of life. All organisms are made up of one or many cells.

cellulose (SELL-yu-lohz): a large molecule made up of a long chain of sugar molecules that forms the main structure of wood and plant cell walls

decomposer (dee-kuhm-POH-zer): an organism that breaks down dead plants or animals

detritus (dee-TRAHY-tuhs): decaying bits of plants and animals

ecosystem (EE-coh-sis-tum): a community of plants, animals, and other organisms and the environment they live in

exoskeleton (ex-oh-SKELL-eh-tun): the tough outer covering of insects and other arthropods

frass (FRAS): the waste and debris produced by insects

fruiting body (FROO-ting BAH-dee): the reproductive part of fungi or slime molds

gravity (GRAV-uh-tee): a force that attracts any two objects to each other, especially the force that makes objects fall toward the center of Earth

humus (YU-miss): the nutrient-rich part of soil made from dead organisms and living microbes

kingdom (KING-duhm): a major group of living organisms, such as animals, plants, or bacteria

larva (LAHR-vah): the second stage of an insect with four life stages; plural, larvae (LAHR-vay)

lichen (LAHY-ken): an organism made up of two organisms—a fungus and an alga

microbe (MY-krohb): a microscopic single-celled organism

molecule (MOL-uh-kyool): the smallest unit of a substance

mycelium (mahy-SEEL-ee-um): the main body of the fungus made up of multiple fibers; plural, mycelia

nucleus (NU-clee-us): a structure in a cell that controls reproduction and growth

nutrient (NEW-tree-uhnt): a chemical that feeds organisms and helps them to grow

organism (OR-gun-iz-um): a single individual of any form of life

outer bark (OW-ter BARK): the dead, protective layer on the outside of a tree trunk

phloem (FLOHM): the portion of the inner bark that transports sugar and nutrients dissolved in sap from the leaves to the rest of the plant

plasmodium (plaz-MOH-dee-um): a bloblike form of a slime mold made of a single cell and many nuclei that move about by streaming

protist (PROH-tist): a single-celled or simple organism generally larger than bacteria and having a more complex cell structure

pupa (PEW-puh): the inactive third stage of an insect with four life stages. Inside the pupa, larval structures break down and adult structures develop.

pupate (PEW-payt): to change from a larva to a pupa

secretion (suh-CREE-shun): a substance made and released by a bodily organ

species (SPEE-seez): a single kind of plant, animal, or other organism

xylem (ZAY-lum): the woody center of trunks and stems that carries water and minerals from the roots up to the rest of the tree

FURTHER INFORMATION

BOOKS

Crow-Miller, Britt. *World of Rot: Learn All About the Wriggly, Slimy, Super-Cool Decomposers We Couldn't Live Without*. Illustrated by Bruno Valasse. Storey, 2024. Investigate the science of decay and look at the organisms doing the dirty work.

Holland, Mary. *Snag It: Who Needs a Dead Tree?* Arbordale, 2025. Like logs, standing dead trees are inhabited by many decomposers and animals seeking shelter.

Pendreigh, Kirsten. *When a Tree Falls: Nurse Logs and Their Incredible Forest Power*. Illustrated by Elke Boschinger. Chronicle Books, 2025. When a tree falls in the Pacific Northwest, it becomes home to numerous animals and plants including young trees getting their start on the log.

Sanchez, Anita. *Rotten! Vultures, Beetles, Slime, and Nature's Other Decomposers*. Illustrated by Gilbert Ford. Houghton Mifflin Harcourt, 2019. This is a funny, fact-filled exploration of the many decomposers and their important role in the environment.

WEBSITES AND VIDEOS

Bug Chicks Video: Bess Beetles and Introducing "The Daily Antenna"
https://thebugchicks.com/articles/arthropods/bess-beetles-and-introducing-the-daily-antenna-2?rq=beetle
Learn about the family life, communication, and feeding habits of one of the most unusual beetles that calls rotten logs its home.

The Homeschool Scientist: Life Under a Log
https://thehomeschoolscientist.com/life-under-a-log/
Explores some of the organisms found under logs and how they fit into their environment. Two videos are included. One investigates what lives under logs in California. The other explains the role of decomposers and how they fit into the food chain.

"Life Under a Rotting Log! Lake Lynn Park"
https://www.youtube.com/watch?v=9tVRFHJfXYM
Laurie Nielsen from Raleigh, North Carolina, Parks and Recreation shows us how to look for animals under logs, what can be found, and their special features.

Ottawa Field Naturalists' Club: The Importance of Snags and Downed Logs to Wildlife
https://ofnc.ca/conservation-how-to/the-importance-of-snags-and-downed-logs-to-wildlife
Find out why dead trees are so important to wildlife, whether they are still standing or logs on the ground.

Pennsylvania Game Commission: Decomposition Inquisition
https://www.pa.gov/content/dam/copapwp-pagov/en/pgc/documents/education/wildlife-on-wifi/documents/decomposition%20inquisition.pdf
An online guide from the Pennsylvania Game Commission on how to study life in logs. What can you find there? What role does each animal play?

INDEX